This book belongs to:

Learn Sight Words

Say the Word. Fill in the blank, then practice writing.

who
_____ likes ice cream?

who

when
_____ will you be here?

when

them
Can you give the presents
to _____ ?

them

FILL IN THE BLANK SIGHT WORDS

Fill in the sentences using the words in the word bank.
Each word will be used two times.

who	when	them

1. I want to go with _____.

2. _____ can play with me?

3. _____ can we play soccer?

4. _____ is coming to my party?

5. Bring _____ the apples.

6. _____ will it be ready?

Learn Sight Words

Say the Word. Fill in the blank, then practice writing.

★ because

My unicorn will win _____ she is fast.

_____
because
_____
- -
_____

★ just

We got there _____ in time.

_____
just
_____
- -
_____

★ little

The _____ kitten is the cutest.

_____
little
_____
- -
_____

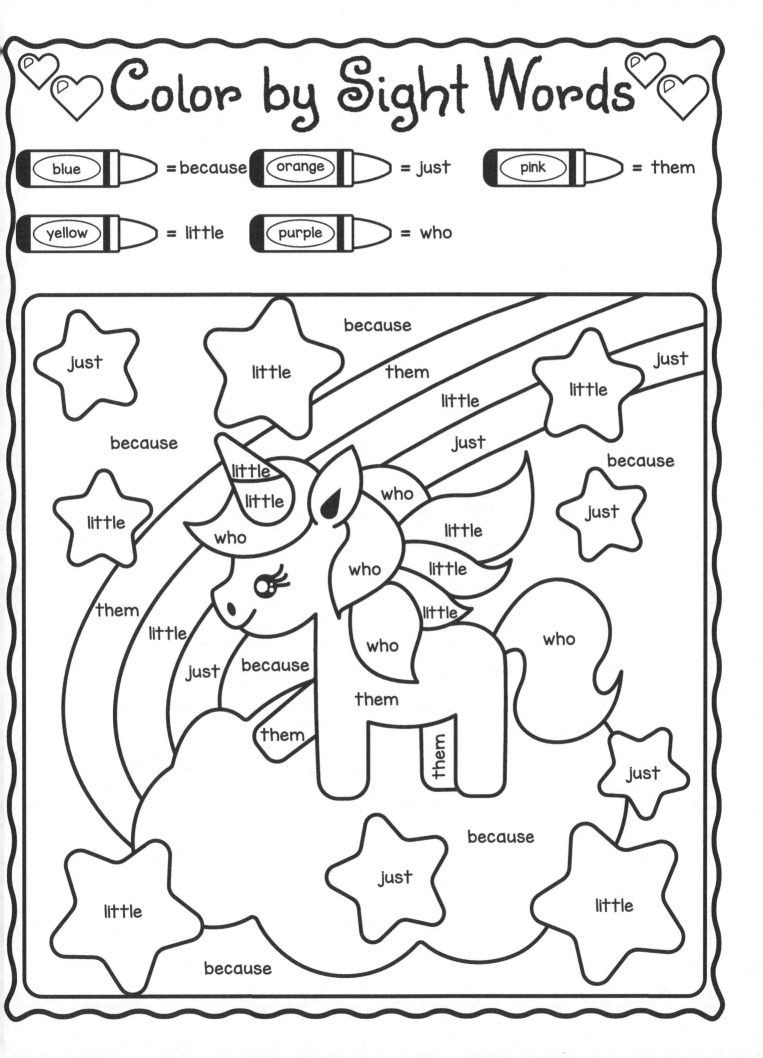

Learn Sight Words

Say the Word. Fill in the blank, then practice writing.

before

Finish your homework

_____ dinner.

before

mother

My _____ is so pretty.

mother

where

_____ can you find a mermaid?

where

WRITE THREE SENTENCES

♥ Say the sight word out loud. Then practice by writing it in a sentence.

before

mother

where

Learn Sight Words

Say the Word. Fill in the blank, then practice writing.

very — That is a _____ big castle.

very _____

_____

could — I wish I _____ fly.

could _____

_____

were — We _____ winning the soccer game.

were _____

_____

SEEK A SIGHT WORD

Read all the sight words. Find the sight words below and color

green = very   red = could   yellow = were

Learn Sight Words

Say the Word. Fill in the blank, then practice writing.

over

Can you jump _____ a rainbow?

over

ride

I want to _____ on a flying unicorn.

ride

don't

I _____ like homework.

don't

FILL IN THE BLANK SIGHT WORDS

Fill in the sentences using the words in the word bank.
Each word will be used two times.

over	ride	don't

1. _____ eat my candy!

2. I went for a _____ on my bike.

3. I _____ want to go to the doctor.

4. Take this _____ to her.

5. He went for a _____ in his boat.

6. Can you come _____ to my

house?

Learn Sight Words

Say the Word. Fill in the blank, then practice writing.

said

The girl _____ hello to me.

said

that

_____ butterfly has big wings.

that

with

I like pink hearts _____ purple spots.

with

Color by Sight Words

blue = said   red = with   pink = over

yellow = that   green = ride

Learn Sight Words

Say the Word. Fill in the blank, then practice writing.

their _____ house is yellow.

their

what _____ is your favorite game to play?

what

but My friend is nice, _____ can be bossy.

but

WRITE THREE SENTENCES

♥ Say the sight word out loud. Then practice by writing it in a sentence.

their

what

but

Learn Sight Words

Say the Word. Fill in the blank, then practice writing.

here _____ is a cute puppy.

here _____

_____

going I am _____ to the end of the rainbow!

going _____

_____

our _____ house has a pretty garden.

our _____

_____

SEEK A SIGHT WORD

Read all the sight words. Find the sight words below and color

blue = here   orange = going   green = our

Learn Sight Words

Say the Word. Fill in the blank, then practice writing.

want

I _____ to swim like
a mermaid.

want

able

The dog is _____
to run fast.

able

bad

I am _____
at waiting.

bad

FILL IN THE BLANK SIGHT WORDS

Fill in the sentences using the words in the word bank.
Each word will be used two times.

want	able	bad

1. I hope she is _____ to go

with us.

2. I _____ a cookie.

3. The _____ dog ate my homework.

4. I _____ a pet cat.

5. My brother was _____

at school.

6. I am ____ to do anything!

Learn Sight Words

Say the Word. Fill in the blank, then practice writing.

give — I want to _____ you a balloon.

give

today — _____ I am going to read a book.

today

week — This _____ there is no school.

week

Learn Sight Words

Say the Word. Fill in the blank, then practice writing.

something

I have _____ exciting to tell you!

something

---

bus

I get to ride the _____ .

bus

---

year

This _____ I want to learn to ice skate.

year

WRITE THREE SENTENCES

♥ Say the sight word out loud. Then practice by writing it in a sentence.

something

bus

year

Learn Sight Words

Say the Word. Fill in the blank, then practice writing.

can't

I _____ do a cartwheel.

can't _____

tell

Can you _____ me a secret?

tell _____

across

The mermaid swims _____ the sea.

across _____

SEEK A SIGHT WORD

Read all the sight words. Find the sight words below and color

red = can't   pink = tell   purple = across

can't

something

across

today

across

tell

able

can't

tell

tell

bad

across

can't

want

Learn Sight Words

Say the Word. Fill in the blank, then practice writing.

world

The _____ is a big place.

world

cat

His _____ is black and white.

cat

take

_____ the apples to the girl.

take

FILL IN THE BLANK SIGHT WORDS

Fill in the sentences using the words in the word bank.
Each word will be used two times.

world	cat	take

1. Will you _____ a picture of me?

2. We need to keep our _____ clean.

3. I have to _____ a test today.

4. My _____ likes to play.

5. The _____ is full of people.

6. The _____ will come in the house.

Learn Sight Words

Say the Word. Fill in the blank, then practice writing.

dad

My _____ likes to play ball with me.

dad

hide

A fox can _____ in his hole.

hide

almost

I can _____ see the rainbow.

almost

Color by Sight Words

Learn Sight Words

Say the Word. Fill in the blank, then practice writing.

dog

The _____ sleeps on the bed.

dog

anything

Is there _____ you want to do?

anything

home

I want to go _____ now please.

home

WRITE THREE SENTENCES

♥ Say the sight word out loud. Then practice by writing it in a sentence.

dog

anything

home

Learn Sight Words

Say the Word. Fill in the blank, then practice writing.

down   Put _____ the cup.

down

become   I want to _____ great!

become

end   I am almost at the _____ of my book.

end

SEEK A SIGHT WORD

Read all the sight words. Find the sight words below and color

yellow = down   blue = become   orange = end

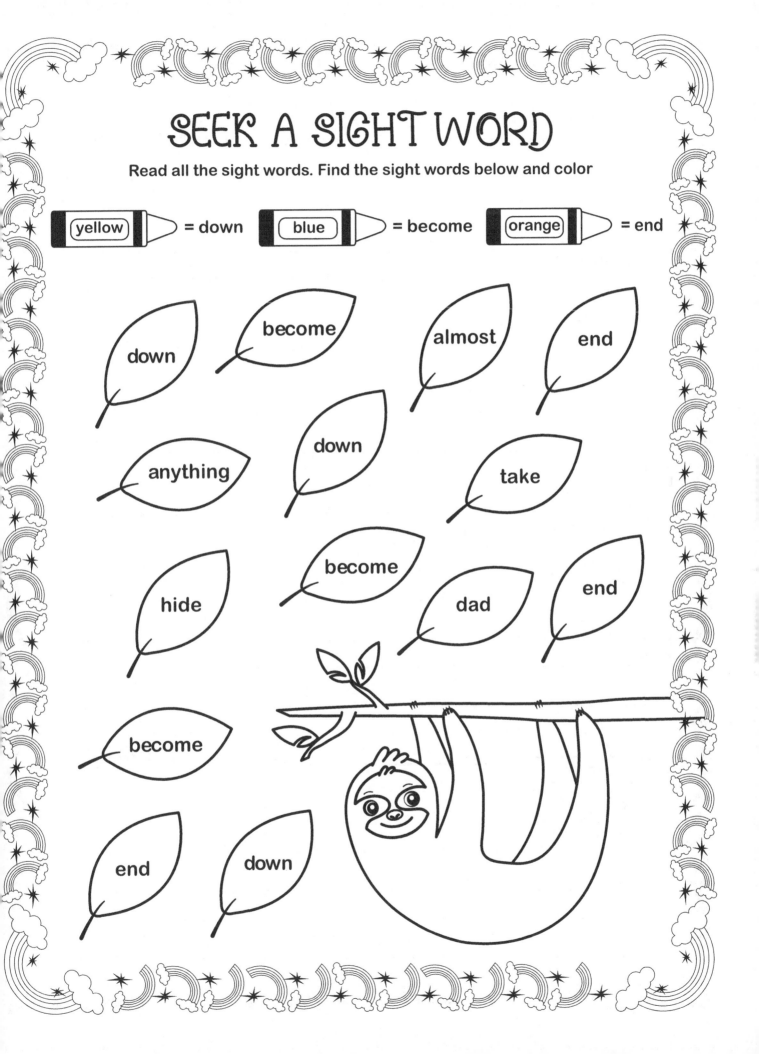

Learn Sight Words

Say the Word. Fill in the blank, then practice writing.

behind

I hid a flower _____ my back to give my mom.

behind

fish

There are lots of _____ in the sea.

fish

why

_____ are you running?

why

FILL IN THE BLANK SIGHT WORDS

Fill in the sentences using the words in the word bank.
Each word will be used two times.

behind	fish	why

1. The mermaid is _____ the kelp.

2. _____ can't we eat the cake?

3. I can catch a _____ in the pond.

4. She is hiding _____ the tree.

5. Please feed my pet _____.

6. _____ did the ladybug fly away?

Learn Sight Words

Say the Word. Fill in the blank, then practice writing.

car

The _____ is red.

car

book

He will read the _____ to her.

book

good

I was _____ at school today.

good

Color by Sight Words

blue = car orange = good pink = why

green = book purple = behind

Learn Sight Words

Say the Word. Fill in the blank, then practice writing.

help

Can you _____ me with my hair?

help

city

I live in the _____

city

write

I will _____ a note to my friend.

write

WRITE THREE SENTENCES

♥ Say the sight word out loud. Then practice by writing it in a sentence.

help

city

write

Learn Sight Words

Say the Word. Fill in the blank, then practice writing.

top

I went to the _____ of the castle.

top

room

Her _____ is pink.

room

under

I went _____ the blanket.

under

SEEK A SIGHT WORD

Read all the sight words. Find the sight words below and color

orange = top   pink = room   purple = under

under

top

help

room

under

good

room

book

car

top

top

why

room

under

Learn Sight Words

Say the Word. Fill in the blank, then practice writing.

fast

I was so _____ in the race.

fast

hill

I ride my bike down the

_____ .

hill

know

I _____ my sight words!

know

FILL IN THE BLANK SIGHT WORDS

Fill in the sentences using the words in the word bank.
Each word will be used two times.

fast	hill	know

1. The horse can run so _____.

2. I_____ my friends will be there.

3. He wants to sled _____ down

the _____.

4. Do you _____ her teacher?

5. The flowers grow on the _____.

Learn Sight Words

Say the Word. Fill in the blank, then practice writing.

use

I can _____ these words in a sentence.

use

let

I _____ the horse have my apple.

let

place

What _____ does she want to go?

place

Color by Sight Words

blue = use

pink = place

orange = fast

purple = let

yellow = know

Learn Sight Words

Say the Word. Fill in the blank, then practice writing.

★ sleep

I want to _____ in my bed.

sleep

★ love

I _____ my mom.

love

★ much

I had too _____ ice cream.

much

WRITE THREE SENTENCES

♥ Say the sight word out loud. Then practice by writing it in a sentence.

sleep

love

much

Learn Sight Words

Say the Word. Fill in the blank, then practice writing.

stay

The butterflies_____ in the garden.

stay

name

What is your _____ ?

name

new

I got a _____ toy.

new

SEEK A SIGHT WORD

Read all the sight words. Find the sight words below and color

red = stay   orange = name   yellow = new

sleep

new

use

name

place

stay

stay

know

new

new

stay

let

name

name

Learn Sight Words

Say the Word. Fill in the blank, then practice writing.

paper

She got a purple _____ to color.

paper

rain

Let's play in the _____ !

rain

door

The _____ is open.

door

FILL IN THE BLANK SIGHT WORDS

Fill in the sentences using the words in the word bank.
Each word will be used two times.

paper	rain	door

1. We will not have a picnic in the

_____.

2. The boy can hang the _____

on the wall.

3. That house has a yellow _____.

4. Close the _____ when you

come inside.

5. She left her toy out in the _____.

6. Write your name on your _____.

Learn Sight Words

Say the Word. Fill in the blank, then practice writing.

fun

Playing with you is _____ .

fun

sky

The _____ is blue.

sky

both

I like _____ cupcakes and ice cream.

both

Learn Sight Words

Say the Word. Fill in the blank, then practice writing.

time

It is _____ for us to go.

time

sea

The mermaid swims in the _____ .

sea

wrote

He _____ down his name.

wrote

WRITE THREE SENTENCES

♥ Say the sight word out loud. Then practice by writing it in a sentence.

time

see

wrote

Learn Sight Words

Say the Word. Fill in the blank, then practice writing.

again

I want to do it _____ !

again

carry

I can _____ the flowers.

carry

wait

I can't _____ for Spring.

wait

SEEK A SIGHT WORD

Read all the sight words. Find the sight words below and color

yellow = again   pink = carry   purple = wait

again

time

wrote

wait

both

again

wait

carry

wait

carry

fun

carry

sky

again

carry

Learn Sight Words

Say the Word. Fill in the blank, then practice writing.

each

I want a dress in _____ color.

each

feel

I _____ happy today.

feel

always

I will_____ do my best!

always

FILL IN THE BLANK SIGHT WORDS

Fill in the sentences using the words in the word bank.
Each word will be used two times.

each	feel	always

1. I _____ feed my dog.

2. She watered _____ flower

pot.

3. Does it _____ cold in here?

4. Can I try one of _____

cupcake?

5. I can _____ the rabbit's

soft fur.

6. He _____ runs fast.

Learn Sight Words

Say the Word. Fill in the blank, then practice writing.

first

I see the _____ star in the sky.

first

ask

I will _____ if I can go.

ask

food

What kind of _____ does a caticorn eat?

food

Color by Sight Words

green = first   orange = food   pink = each

yellow = ask   blue = always

Learn Sight Words

Say the Word. Fill in the blank, then practice writing.

work

I will _____ hard to learn my words.

work

brother

Her _____ is funny.

brother

though

I want ice cream even _____ it is cold outside.

though

WRITE THREE SENTENCES

♥ Say the sight word out loud. Then practice by writing it in a sentence.

work

brother

though

Learn Sight Words

Say the Word. Fill in the blank, then practice writing.

funny

That dog has a _____ bark.

funny

gave

I _____ my lollipop to him.

gave

thing

Put that _____ in your desk.

thing

SEEK A SIGHT WORD

Read all the sight words. Find the sight words below and color

purple = funny   pink = gave   yellow = thing

each

always

gave

thing

first

funny

ask

funny

gave

thing

thing

though

gave

funny

Learn Sight Words

Say the Word. Fill in the blank, then practice writing.

close

Please _____ the door.

close _____

even

You can do it, _____ if it is hard!

even _____

grow

The garden will _____ pink and red flowers.

grow _____

FILL IN THE BLANK SIGHT WORDS

Fill in the sentences using the words in the word bank.
Each word will be used two times.

close	even	grow

1. The mermaid will _____ her hair

out long.

2. The castle gate will _____ when the

sun goes down.

3. Make sure everyone has an _____

number of papers.

4. The puppy will _____ to be a big dog.

5. The pirate is _____ to the treasure.

6. The girl likes to play in the snow, _____

if it is cold out.

Learn Sight Words

Say the Word. Fill in the blank, then practice writing.

gone

The birds have _____ south for the winter.

gone

same

She has the _____ dress as me.

same

knew

I _____ you would be my friend.

knew

Color by Sight Words

green = gone   orange = knew   yellow = close

blue = same   red = even

Learn Sight Words

Say the Word. Fill in the blank, then practice writing.

begin

I am going to _____
ice skating.

begin

winter

I like for it to snow in the
_____ .

winter

must

He _____ take the
test today.

must

WRITE THREE SENTENCES

♥ Say the sight word out loud. Then practice by writing it in a sentence.

begin

winter

must

Learn Sight Words

Say the Word. Fill in the blank, then practice writing.

stop

Can you _____ doing that?

stop

happy

I am _____ when I sing.

happy

catch

She will _____ the ball.

catch

SEEK A SIGHT WORD

Read all the sight words. Find the sight words below and color

pink = stop   green = happy   orange = catch

Learn Sight Words

Say the Word. Fill in the blank, then practice writing.

third   We got _____ place in the contest.

third

night   I like to see fireflies at _____ .

night

goes   The rainbow _____ across the sky.

goes

FILL IN THE BLANK SIGHT WORDS

Fill in the sentences using the words in the word bank.
Each word will be used two times.

third	night	goes

1- He is on _____ base in the ball game.

2- We are going to sleep in a tent at _____.

3- That is the _____ time I have said that.

4- The boy _____ skating in the park.

5- Always brush your teeth in the morning and at _____.

6- There _____ a butterfly!

Learn Sight Words

Say the Word. Fill in the blank, then practice writing.

last

That is the _____ time I will do that!

last

school

I love to learn at

_____ .

school

walk

Let's go for a _____ in the sun.

walk

Color by Sight Words

purple = last
orange = walk
pink = goes
blue = school
yellow = night

Learn Sight Words

Say the Word. Fill in the blank, then practice writing.

ten

I have _____ fingers and _____ toes.

ten _____

change

We can _____ the world and make it better!

change _____

outside

I love to play _____.

outside _____

WRITE THREE SENTENCES

♥ Say the sight word out loud. Then practice by writing it in a sentence.

ten

change

outside

Learn Sight Words

Say the Word. Fill in the blank, then practice writing.

part _____ of our class wants pink cake and the other wants green.

part

live Worms_____in the garden.

live

party I am having ice cream at my _____

party

SEEK A SIGHT WORD

Read all the sight words. Find the sight words below and color

red = part   pink = live   purple = party

night

party

live

change

part

part

school

goes

part

live

party

last

party

live

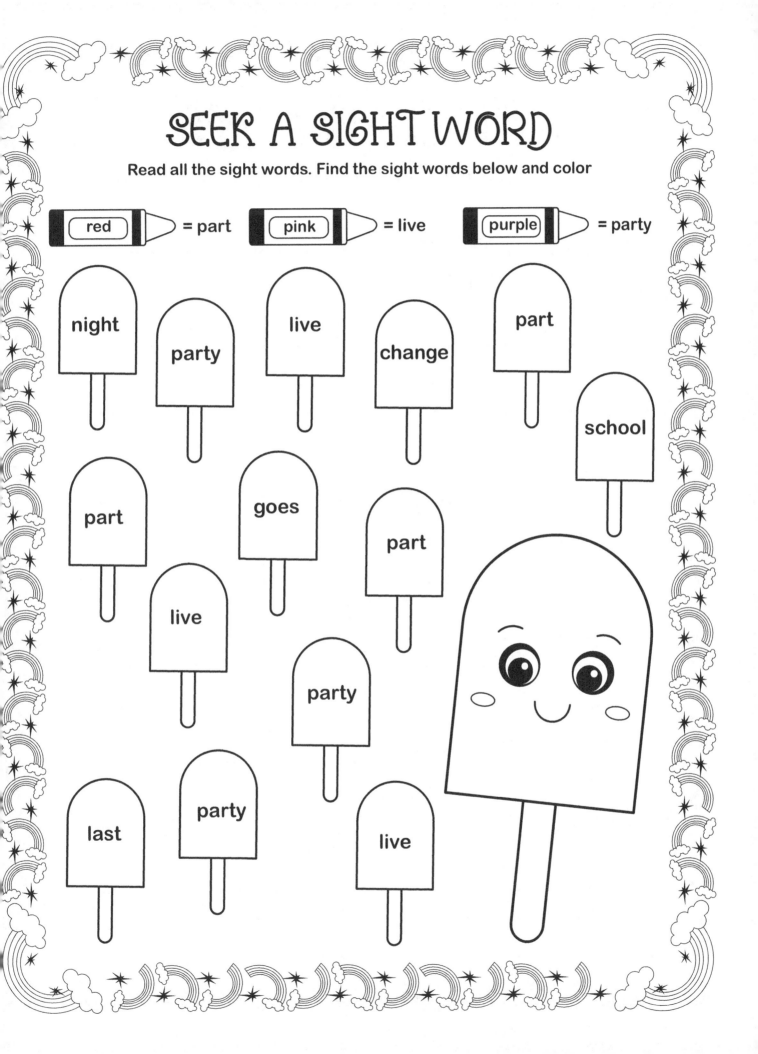

Learn Sight Words

Say the Word. Fill in the blank, then practice writing.

game

Will you play a _____ with us?

game

try

I will _____ to do my best!

try

pick

He will _____ us for the team.

pick

FILL IN THE BLANK SIGHT WORDS

Fill in the sentences using the words in the word bank.
Each word will be used two times.

game	try	pick

1. _____ up your pencils

and let's begin.

2. We will go get pizza after the

_____.

3. Will you _____ to be more quiet?

4. The fairy will _____ up

the seeds to plant flowers.

5. Always give it your best _____.

6. I scored a goal during the _____.

Learn Sight Words

Say the Word. Fill in the blank, then practice writing.

right

Will you feed the dog

_____ **now?**

right _____

until

We play inside _____

it stops raining.

until _____

second

I would like a _____

scoop of ice cream.

second _____

Color by Sight Words

red = right

orange = second

blue = try

yellow = until

pink = game

Learn Sight Words

Say the Word. Fill in the blank, then practice writing.

does _____ this flower smell nice?

does

together Let's go to the park _____ .

together

house The blue _____ has a big garden.

house

WRITE THREE SENTENCES

♥ Say the sight word out loud. Then practice by writing it in a sentence.

does

_____

- - - - - - - - - - - - - - -

_____

- - - - - - - - - - - - - - -

_____

together

_____

- - - - - - - - - - - - - - -

_____

- - - - - - - - - - - - - - -

_____

house

_____

- - - - - - - - - - - - - - -

_____

- - - - - - - - - - - - - - -

_____

Learn Sight Words

Say the Word. Fill in the blank, then practice writing.

start

The race is about to

_____ .

start

grew

They _____ apple
trees in the yard.

grew

way

Which _____ did
the dog go?

way

SEEK A SIGHT WORD

Read all the sight words. Find the sight words below and color

pink = start   blue = grew   green = way

try

grew

start

right

way

way

start

grew

until

way

start

does

grew

together

Learn Sight Words

Say the Word. Fill in the blank, then practice writing.

deep

The mermaid lives

_____ in the sea.

deep

view

I have a pretty _____

when I fly on my unicorn.

view

snow

Let's make a fort in the

_____ .

snow

FILL IN THE BLANK SIGHT WORDS

Fill in the sentences using the words in the word bank.
Each word will be used two times.

deep   view   snow

1. I am afraid to swim in the _____

end of the pool.

2. After we play in the _____,

I like to drink hot chocolate.

3. I can see a good _____ from

my treehouse.

4. We will not got to school if there is

_____ tomorrow.

5. She had a _____ of the

town from on top of the building.

6. I will dig a _____ hole to plant the tree.

Learn Sight Words

Say the Word. Fill in the blank, then practice writing.

friends

Two _____ are coming over to play.

friends

story

My mom will tell us a bedtime _____.

story

street

We will ride our bikes on the _____.

street

Learn Sight Words

Say the Word. Fill in the blank, then practice writing.

above

We looked at the stars

_____ us in the sky.

above

find

I want to _____
a four leaf clover in the grass.

find

between

The birds are flying

_____ the clouds.

between

WRITE THREE SENTENCES

♥ Say the sight word out loud. Then practice by writing it in a sentence.

above

find

between

Learn Sight Words

Say the Word. Fill in the blank, then practice writing.

every

I have read _____ book in that stack.

every

should

You _____ always brush your teeth before bedtime.

should

father

My _____ is bringing us a treat.

father

SEEK A SIGHT WORD

Read all the sight words. Find the sight words below and color

yellow = every   pink = should   orange = father

between

friends

father

should

great

should

father

every

father

every

every

find

should

above

Learn Sight Words

Say the Word. Fill in the blank, then practice writing.

watch _____ me do a flip!

watch

children All of the _____
want to play on the slide.

children

enough Is there _____
ice cream for her, too?

enough

FILL IN THE BLANK SIGHT WORDS

Fill in the sentences using the words in the word bank.
Each word will be used two times.

watch children enough

1. The _____ are playing

with the ball.

2. Does the cat have _____ water?

3. I want to _____ that show.

4. I don't have _____ money

for that.

5. We will _____ the birds flying.

6. All of the _____ come to

school.

Learn Sight Words

Say the Word. Fill in the blank, then practice writing.

★ **dark**

If the room is _____ turn on the light.

dark _____

_____

★ **great**

It is _____ to be a kid!

great _____

_____

★ **inside**

Come _____ when you get cold.

inside _____

_____

Learn Sight Words

Say the Word. Fill in the blank, then practice writing.

light

That _____ in the sky is a star.

light

seen

Have you _____ her today?

seen

during

Please do not talk _____ class.

during

WRITE THREE SENTENCES

♥ Say the sight word out loud. Then practice by writing it in a sentence.

light

seen

during

Learn Sight Words

Say the Word. Fill in the blank, then practice writing.

wrong — It is _____ that he took your toy.

wrong

you're — _____ such a nice person.

you're

several — I am going to play with _____ of my friends.

several

SEEK A SIGHT WORD

Read all the sight words. Find the sight words below and color

blue = wrong   green = you're   yellow = several

seen

several

you're

you're

during

wrong

several

light

several

wrong

dark

you're

enough

wrong

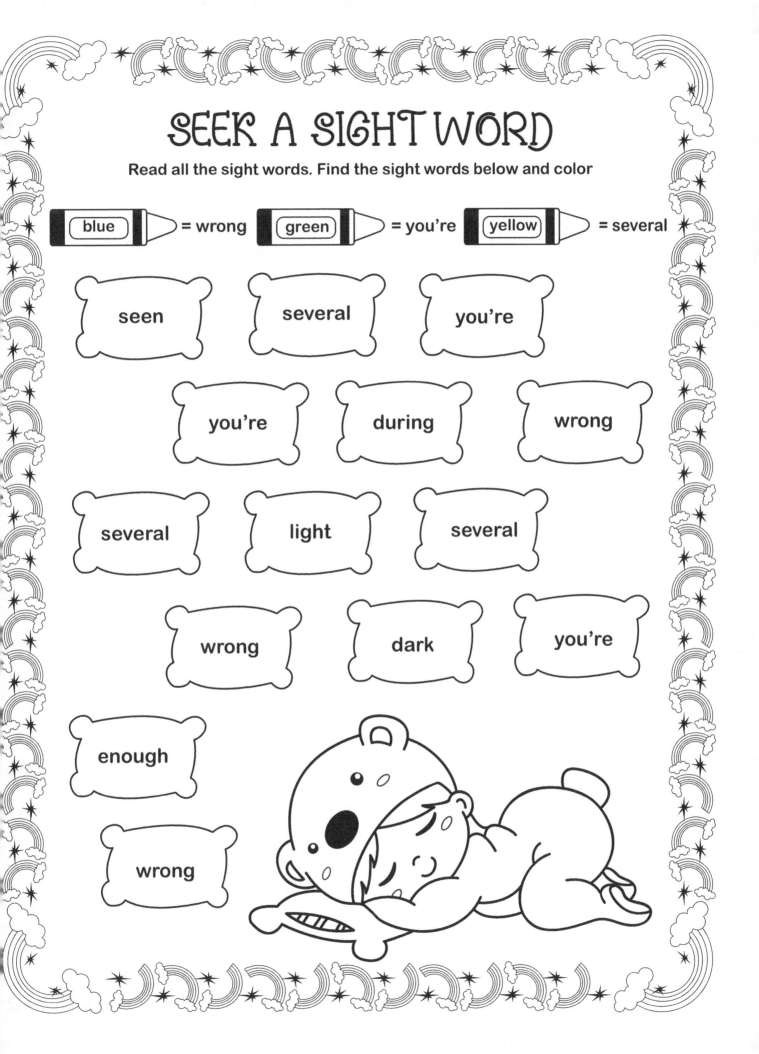

Learn Sight Words

Say the Word. Fill in the blank, then practice writing.

never

I am _____ doing that again!

never

getting

I do not like _____ up in the morning.

getting

earth

Our _____ has land and water on it.

earth

FILL IN THE BLANK SIGHT WORDS

Fill in the sentences using the words in the word bank.
Each word will be used two times.

never   getting   earth

1. We need to take care of our

_____.

2. You should _____

put trash on the ground.

3. I am _____ a gift

for my birthday.

4. _____ let your dog

eat your homework!

5. The _____ is round.

6. We are _____ a new dog.

Learn Sight Words

Say the Word. Fill in the blank, then practice writing.

group

There is a _____

of kids that want to play tag.

group

baby

The _____ needs his

mom.

baby

everything

_____ in the toy store

looks fun!

everything

Color by Sight Words

brown = group orange = everything pink = earth

yellow = baby green = never

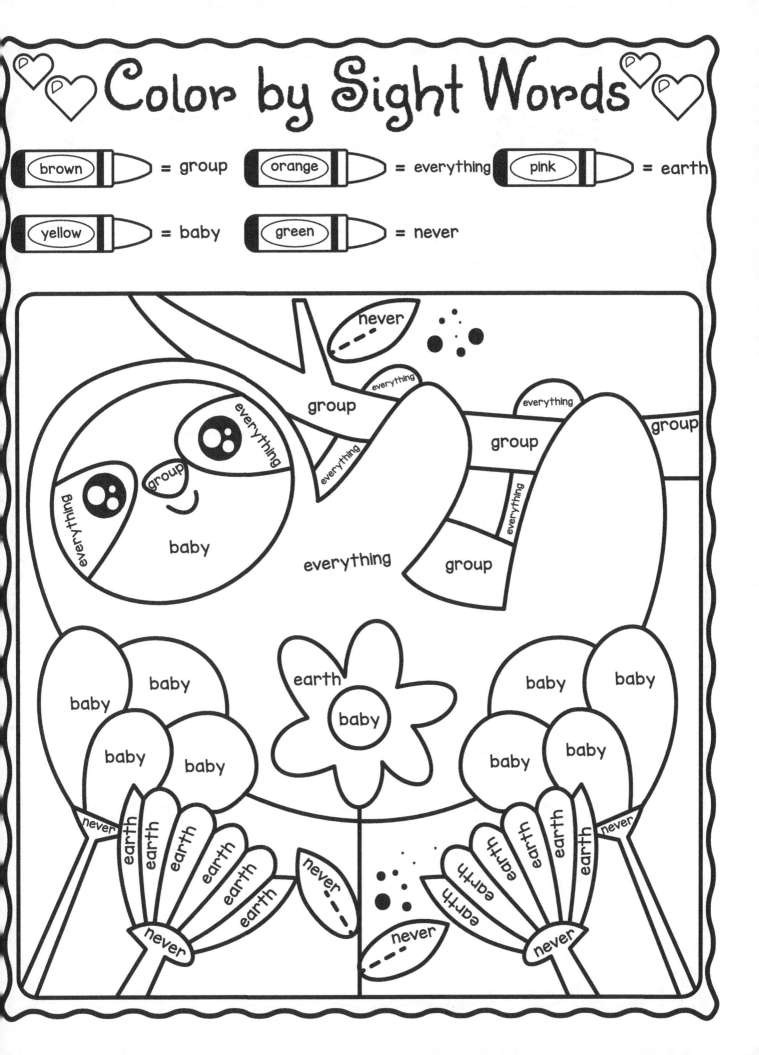

Learn Sight Words

Say the Word. Fill in the blank, then practice writing.

high

She pushed me _____
on the swings.

high

wouldn't

The cat _____
come near the dogs.

wouldn't

probably

Mom says I _____
should not eat ice cream for dinner!

probably

WRITE THREE SENTENCES

♥ Say the sight word out loud. Then practice by writing it in a sentence.

high

_____

_____

_____

wouldn't

_____

_____

_____

probably

_____

_____

_____

Learn Sight Words

Say the Word. Fill in the blank, then practice writing.

★ through

Put your feet _____ the hoop.

through

★ against

My bike is leaning _____ the house.

against

★ hours

It is only three _____ until we leave on our trip.

hours

SEEK A SIGHT WORD

Read all the sight words. Find the sight words below and color

blue ▷ = through   pink ▷ = against   orange ▷ = hours

wouldn't

never   against   through

through   hours   everything   hours

getting   hours   probably   against

against   through

Learn Sight Words

Say the Word. Fill in the blank, then practice writing.

fight

The dog and the cat got into a

_____ .

f i g h t _____

_____

once

I have to get up early, but

_____ a week I get

to sleep in late.

o n c e _____

_____

best

I am the _____

speller in my class.

b e s t _____

_____

FILL IN THE BLANK SIGHT WORDS

Fill in the sentences using the words in the word bank.
Each word will be used two times.

fight   once   best

1. Her mom makes the _____ apple pie.

2. _____ upon a time, a princess

lived in a castle.

3. The ants are going to _____

over that food.

4. You can have a treat, _____

we finish our shopping.

5. It was a hard _____ to win

that race.

6. She is the _____ runner I have

ever seen.

Learn Sight Words

Say the Word. Fill in the blank, then practice writing.

ready Are you _____ to go?

ready

free We won _____ tickets to go see a movie.

free

show I want to _____ you what I can do.

show

Learn Sight Words

Say the Word. Fill in the blank, then practice writing.

★ building

The man works in that

_____ .

building

★ draw

Will you _____ a picture for me?

draw

★ state

That _____ gets a lot of snow in the winter.

state

WRITE THREE SENTENCES

♥ Say the sight word out loud. Then practice by writing it in a sentence.

building

draw

state

Learn Sight Words

Say the Word. Fill in the blank, then practice writing.

kind

Always be _____ to people.

kind

circle

The girls sat in a _____ around the fire.

circle

large

That _____ cat is a tiger.

large

SEEK A SIGHT WORD

Read all the sight words. Find the sight words below and color

purple = kind   orange = circle   pink = large

once   large   circle

best   large   circle

large   kind   free

kind

building

show

kind

circle

Learn Sight Words

Say the Word. Fill in the blank, then practice writing.

doing

What are you _____ after school?

doing _____

_____

family

My _____ is going to the beach.

family _____

_____

clothes

Pack your _____ in this bag.

clothes _____

_____

FILL IN THE BLANK SIGHT WORDS

Fill in the sentences using the words in the word bank.
Each word will be used two times.

doing   family   clothes

1. The boy's _____ got dirty in

the mud.

2. A bird _____ lives in the nest.

3. They are _____ a cheer to

get the team ready.

4. A new _____ moved in

next door.

5. I got new _____ for the

party.

6. After _____ my homework,

I will play outside.

Learn Sight Words

Say the Word. Fill in the blank, then practice writing.

⭐ hand

Will you _____ her the toy?

hand _____

⭐ different

I will pick a _____ color dress than she has.

different _____

⭐ river

We took the boat out on the _____ .

river _____

Learn Sight Words

Say the Word. Fill in the blank, then practice writing.

might

She _____ come over to play later.

might

air

The birds flew in the _____.

air

I'd

_____ like a pink cupcake, please!

I'd

WRITE THREE SENTENCES

♥ Say the sight word out loud. Then practice by writing it in a sentence.

might

air

I'd

Learn Sight Words

Say the Word. Fill in the blank, then practice writing.

suddenly   The mermaid swam away
_____ .

suddenly

easy   This work is _____ because
I am so smart!

easy

finally   It _____ got dark
and we could see the stars.

finally

SEEK A SIGHT WORD

Read all the sight words. Find the sight words below and color

orange = suddenly   red = easy   pink = finally

family

hold

finally

easy

everyone

easy

finally

doing

suddenly

finally

easy

suddenly

suddenly

I'd

Learn Sight Words

Say the Word. Fill in the blank, then practice writing.

everyone

Can you ask _____ to come over here?

everyone

hold

_____ the butterfly with lots of care.

hold

special

This is my _____ teddy bear.

special

FILL IN THE BLANK SIGHT WORDS

Fill in the sentences using the words in the word bank.
Each word will be used two times.

everyone hold special

1. Will you _____ my ball when it is my turn?

2. My family is _____ to me.

3. _____ at the party got some candy.

4. The girl made a _____ card for her mom.

5. The town will _____ a meeting at the park.

6. The waves got _____ on the boat wet

Learn Sight Words

Say the Word. Fill in the blank, then practice writing.

animal

My favorite _____ is a unicorn!

animal

lost

The little boy was _____ from his family.

lost

beautiful

The _____ flower grows in the garden.

beautiful

Learn Sight Words

Say the Word. Fill in the blank, then practice writing.

need   I _____ you to pick up the books for me.

need

job   It is a big _____ to learn all these words!

job

maybe   If you come over, _____ we can play a game.

maybe

WRITE THREE SENTENCES

♥ Say the sight word out loud. Then practice by writing it in a sentence.

need

_____

_____

_____

_____

job

_____

_____

_____

_____

maybe

_____

_____

_____

_____

Made in the USA
Monee, IL
05 April 2022

94203287R00077